OPTIONS TRADING

FOR BEGINNERS

Trade for a living and earn extra passive income. Invest from home, learn how to swing trade stocks. Tips on risk management. Get financial freedom with a positive ROI in 7 days

MARK BROKER

© **Copyright 2020 - All rights reserved.**

The content contained within this book may not be reproduced, duplicated or transmitted without direct written permission from the author or the publisher.

Under no circumstances will any blame or legal responsibility be held against the publisher, or author, for any damages, reparation, or monetary loss due to the information contained within this book. Either directly or indirectly.

Legal Notice:

This book is copyright protected. This book is only for personal use. You cannot amend, distribute, sell, use, quote or paraphrase any part, or the content within this book, without the consent of the author or publisher.

Disclaimer Notice:

Please note the information contained within this document is for educational and entertainment purposes only. All effort has been executed to present accurate, up to date, and reliable, complete information. No warranties of any kind are declared or implied. Readers acknowledge that the author is not engaging in the rendering of legal, financial, medical or professional advice. The content within this book has been derived from various sources. Please consult a licensed professional before attempting any techniques outlined in this book.

By reading this document, the reader agrees that under no circumstances is the author responsible for any losses, direct or indirect, which are incurred as a result of the use of information contained within this document, including, but not limited to, — errors, omissions, or inaccuracies.

TABLE OF CONTENTS

INTRODUCTION 1
1. OPTIONS TRADING BASICS 3
   What Options Trading is? 3
      Uses of Options 4
      Derivatives 4
   Options Trading Characteristics 5
      All Options Expire 5
      All Options Have a Strike Price 5
      Option Contract Multiplier 5
   Types of Options 6
   What is Call? What is Put? 7
   Buying and Selling 8
2. WHY TRADE WITH OPTIONS 10
   The Benefits of Options Trading 10
      Options have Low Risk 10
      Options are More Cost-Effective 11
   Options Offer Higher Returns 13
   More Alternatives with Options 13
   Why Options are a Better Choice? 14
      Hedging 14
      Speculation 14
   How does Options Trading work? 15
   Types of Options 17
   Options Liquidity & Expiry Time 17
   How to Read Options Table? 18
3. MAJOR OPTION TRADING CONCEPTS 20
   History of Option Trading 21
   Risks In Options Trading? 22
      Different Strategies Used In Option Trading 22
      Stock VS Option 23
      Option Trading Platforms 23
   Option Practicing Method 24
   Strategies for option trading 25
   The Worth of Option Trading 27

Option Trading VS Stock Trading 28
Risk in Option Trading 29
    Option Account 29
What Is An Option Account? 29
    The Right Broker 30
    The Best Broker 30
Best platforms 30

4. OPTIONS TRADING MYTHS AND MISCONCEPTIONS 32
5. TOP OPTIONS TRADING STRATEGIES 37
Buying calls 37
Buying puts 38
Covered call 39
    Iron condors 41
Bear calls 42
Jade lizard 43
Collar option 44
Diagonal spread 45
Butterfly 46

6. TOP QUALITIES OF A SUCCESSFUL OPTIONS TRADER 48
Options Trading 48
    Why people tend to go for options trading? 48
Top Qualities of a Successful Options Trader 49
    Control on Emotions 50
    Records Management 50
    A Good Planner 50
    Consistency 51
    Learning from Failures 51
    News Interpretation 52
    Do not Follow What Others are Doing 52
    Patience 52
    Flexibility 53
    Risk Management 53
    Conclusion 53

7. HOW TO SELECT THE RIGHT OPTION FOR A MAJOR GAIN
.... 55

Look for the Right Option 55
Frame your Purpose 56
Trader's Payoff 56
Analyze Volatility 57
Recognize Events 57
Make Your Strategy 58
Launch Parameters 58
How to make money with Options Trading 59
    Recap 59
Making Money with Options Trading in 2020 62
    Naked Call 62
    Covered Put 63
Making most out of options 63
Indirect Strategies: 64
Mental strategies: 64

8. IMPORTANT TIPS & TRICKS ABOUT OPTIONS TRADING. 66
Follow a Well Defined Exit Plan 67
    Educate Yourself 68
    Don't Double Up for Past Losses 68
    Manage Your Risk 69
    Finally 70

9. IMPORTANT FAQS OF OPTIONS TRADING 71
Is there any definition of options? 71
How to gain maximum profit in options trading? 71
What happens in a case when options contract expires? 72
What is the difference between strike price and stock price? 72
What is naked call? 73
What is American contract? 73
What is an European contract? 73
Which one is more profitable European contract or American contract? 73
So an American style contract is exercised more but is it more profitable? 74
    When should you start options trading? 74
    How much should you invest in options trading? 74
    When should you exercise your options? 74

Best strategy of options trading?.. 75
What is a short put and long call strategy? 75
How an option writer makes money?... 75
How do investors lose money in options trading? 75
CONCLUSION..**77**

INTRODUCTION

Out of many misconceptions, one that surrounds many markets is options are risky. Well, if you ask an options trader, he won't agree to this. The reason is if options trading were risky, it would have been an obsolete concept in the market. Why are more and more traders and investors jumping into this business?

There is just fear that makes people think that options are not profitable. All you need to do is grab all the concepts carefully and apply them when needed. Moreover, make sure you pick the right strategy and at the right time.

"Investing should be more like watching paint dry or watching grass grow. If you want excitement, take $800 and go to Las Vegas." - Paul Samuelson

Have some patience since investment is no joke! According to a ballpark estimate, a beginner needs at least one to two years to become a highly successful trader.

You can rely on this beginners' guide book on options trading that contains all the basic concepts, tips, techniques, solutions related to options trading. Read the theory carefully and then implement the concepts given in it one by one. Here is an authentic mantra to options trading:

Whenever you make a trading strategy, think it through at least three times before your final call – this is the real recipe to success!

1. OPTIONS TRADING BASICS

"Never invest in a business you cannot understand," says Warren Buffett, the famous American Investor, and we agree to him! That's why we shall start from scratch for you in this book.

In this chapter, you will learn the basics of Options Trading with examples. We suggest you take notes of the new concepts you come across in here so you could absorb more than expected.

Here is a Pro Tip: Focus on the concepts and terms given in this. This will help you grab the basics really well. So, shall we start?

What Options Trading is?

At first, options trading looks overpowering, but it is very easy to understand if you start from scratch. By that we mean if you start from concept to concept.

Basically, traders' portfolios are created with different asset categories. For instance, they may be ETFs, stocks, mutual funds, and bonds, etcetera. Options are sort of an asset category with many frills. Meaning, they can give you more benefits than ETFs and stocks.

Uses of Options

Options can make a trader powerful. It is because they can add to a trader's income, leverage, and protection. For every investor, there is an option scenario present. For instance, one can use options as a beneficial hedge against a falling stock market in order to limit the losses. They can also be utilized to make recurring earnings. Besides, options are also used for 'speculative purposes' like betting on the movement of stocks, etcetera.

With bonds and stocks, there isn't anything such as free lunch. Options are also not different. It involves risk, and investors should be well-aware of this.

Derivatives

Derivatives are considered as a 'bigger' group of securities – and options belong to them. A derivative's price is 'derived' from something else. For instance, ketchup is the derivate of tomatoes, and fries are the derivative of potatoes. Similarly, a stock option is the derivate of stocks, while options are derived from financial securities.

Some of the examples of derivate include puts, calls, mortgage-backed securities, futures, swaps, forwards, and more.

So, what you understand by options?

- Options are basically contracts. They allow buyers the rights (not obligations) to purchase or sell (in case of a call or put) a specific asset at a certain price or before specified expiry date.

- Investors use them for generating income, hedging risks, or speculating.

- They are called derivatives. The reason is options derive their value from underlying assets.

- A (stock option) contract typically has 100 shares of (an underlying) stock, but they may be written on any type of underlying asset from currencies, bonds to commodities.

Options Trading Characteristics

All Options Expire

Remember, all options expire one day. This means they 'DIE' after the expiration day. This expiry could be after two days or two years. Meaning, traders need to think about the expiry time before buying an option.

Stocks can be held for life, on the other hand.

All Options Have a Strike Price

There is a 'strike price' for every option. This is the prince in which an option can be converted into 'shares of stock.' For instance, if there is a strike price set for an option at $109. You can use the option to buy/sell shares of stock at this strike price.

Option Contract Multiplier

Let us suppose there is a share of stock with a price of $105. It can be purchased at $105. When an option is $6.00, It CANNOT be purchased at $6.00. you would rather need $600 to buy this.

The reason is options can be traded with 100 shares of stock. Meaning, you need to multiply an option price with 100 to attain its 'premium.'

Types of Options

Options trading has immense upward potential with limited risk. There are two main types of Options.

- Call Options

Call option price shows an upward movement when the stock price increases, and it starts to go down when the stock price goes down. Meaning, you can say that it is directly proportional to stock prices.

Call Option Price moves with the Stock price!

One can share 100 shares of stock with the strike price of a Call Option. Let us suppose that there is a rental apartment, and its price is $200,000. You want to purchase this apartment, thinking that its value will be doubled after some time. However, you do not want to pay the full price of this apartment.

What to do?

You can purchase a 'Call Option' for this apartment. This option will allow you to make this purchase (of amount

$200,000) in 24 months. But this process will involve a contract, and you will have to pay for that contract.

This financial contract is known as 'Option.'

So, the strike price of this option will be $200,000 with the expiration date of 24 months. The advantage of this is if the apartment price rises during this period, it won't affect you (you will not have to pay extra on that).

Now, let us imagine that the opposite happens. The price of the apartment does not increase in value. Rather it decreases after 24 months to $150,000.

In this case, you are not forced to buy the apartment because you have the option not to buy it. With the decreased price of $150,000 in mind, you will not opt to purchase it at the strike price of $200,000.

Since you paid for the contract at a minimal price (the contract), you only lose that. Now compare this loss with the option to buy the house by paying the full price at once. You would have lost $200,000 or (at least $50,000), wouldn't you?

What is Call? What is Put?

A call option allows an investor the right to purchase stock, while the put option allows him to sell it. Here is an example of the Call option. A person may be interested in purchasing a new apartment in a new building under construction near his locality.

However, he would only want to pay for it once the construction work is complete.

That person can take advantage of his purchase option. Through option, he can purchase it from the owner in the next four years at (let us say) $400,000 as a down payment. This cost will be called "premium."

Here is a put example. Suppose you buy a home, and with that, you also purchase a homeowner's insurance policy. This policy helps to protect your property against damage. You have to pay a premium for this for a fixed period of time. This premium is highly valuable, and it helps to protect the insurance holder in case of a home accident.

Suppose, instead of an apartment, your asset was index investment or stock. So, if a trader wants to buy insurance on his S & P 500 Index, he can buy put options.

Suppose again that you foresee bear market in the future, and you do not want to lose more than 10 or 11 percent in that Index. If the Index trades at $2800 (for instance), you can buy a put option, which will make you eligible to sell the Index at $2550 at any point before the expiration date.

This will help reduce your loss. Even if the market drops at zero, your loss would not be more than 10 percent, in case you hold the put option.

Buying and Selling

Options allow you to do four things:

- Sell Calls
- Sell Puts
- Buy Calls
- Buy Put

Keep these four scenarios in mind because this is important when you enter the trading business. Purchasing stock offers a long position for investors. But buying a call option can extend your position (it can make it even longer). Short selling offers a shorter position. In an underlying stock, selling an uncovered call also gives a short position.

Similarly, buying puts also makes a short position for you in the underlying stocks. While selling naked puts offers you a longer position.

Remember that buyers of options are known as holders, and sellers of options are known as option 'Writers.'

1. There is no obligation on call and put holders to buy or sell. They have their rights. The only risk for them is to spend money on buying premium.

2. However, it is important to call and put writers to buy and sell in case their option expires. This means they can make more, but they also have a higher risk level than holders.

2. WHY TRADE WITH OPTIONS

Options trading first started in 1973. They can give a lot of benefits to individual traders, though they have a reputation for being risky. Well, you must be thinking, what are those benefits, aren't you? Here is the answer to this.

The Benefits of Options Trading

Although options have been around for quite a time now, most investors still 'fear' using them. The reason is less information and incorrect use. Meaning, if you have good knowledge of all the basics of options (like we are providing here), you are more likely to succeed as an investor.

Individual investors should be aware of the correct usage and benefits of options before blindly following the rumors that options are 'risky.'

Options have Low Risk

Some situations call for high risk for buying options than having equities. However, there are also scenarios when using options trading becomes the best strategy. This also depends on how properly you use them. Options need low financial commitment than equities. Moreover, they are impervious, which promises less risk.

Another quality of options is compared with stocks; options are safer. They are protected by stock-loss order. This order helps to halt losses under a predetermined price indicated by the trader. However, the nature of the order also matters a lot.

Let us suppose a trader purchases a stock investing $50. He does not want to lose more than 10 percent; he places a $45 stop order. It becomes a market order when the stock trades below this price. This order can work during the daytime, not during night time.

For instance, stocks close at $51, but the next day, you hear bad news about stocks like the company owner lies about earnings or there is embezzlement noted. Stocks might open down at $20. If this happens, this price would be the first trade below the investor's stop order price. The trader would sell at this price ($20), locking in the loss.

For his protection, if the trader had bought the put, he would not have suffered from that loss. Options do not close when the market goes down and closes. This happens with stop orders. Meaning, stop orders close if the market shuts down.

Options keep the traders covered 24/7. Stop orders cannot provide insurance 24 hours. This is why options are considered as a 'dependable form of hedging.'

Options are More Cost-Effective

With greater leveraging power, options can help save you a lot of money. You can attain an option position the same as you obtain a stock position. To buy 200 shares of a stock worth $80, you have to pay $16,000, for instance. But if you want to buy double calls worth $20 (representing 100 shares contract), the total expenditure would be $4000. How?

Try this formula: 2 contracts multiply by 100 shares divided by contract x $20 price in the market. You will have an additional $12,000 for use at your discretion.

Although this is not so simple, it requires a good understanding and good strategy. You will need to pick the right call at the right time to buy for mimicking the stock position in the correct manner. This strategy is known as Stock Replacement, which is not only viable but also cost-effective and practical.

Let's suppose you want to buy Schlumberger (SLB, thinking that it might increase in value in the next few months. You think you should buy 200 shares and the company is trading at $131. So, your overlay would be $26,200.

Instead of investing such a heavy amount, you could pick options to mimic the stocks and buy a call option called, August – using only a $100 strike price for $34.

If you want to acquire a position equal to the size of 200 shares that are mentioned above, you need to purchase double contracts. Your total investment for this would be $6,800, instead of $26,200. (Here is how: double contacts x 100 shares/contract x market price of $34). You can also get interested on this or use your money for another investment.

Options Offer Higher Returns

Options trading promises higher percentage returns. Traders do not need a calculator to find this. They can invest a low amount and get a higher amount back.

Let us consider the above use case to compare the return on investment. Traders need to purchase stocks for $50 and an option for $6. Suppose options price changes by 80 percent (of the stock price). If stocks move up to $5.5, a trader will get a 10 percent return. But the option would gain 80 percent of the stock price of $4.5. A return of this kind on $6 investment amounts to 67.5 percent, which is much better than a 10 percent profit on stocks.

More Alternatives with Options

Traders can find more investing alternatives with options. They are highly flexible. There are many strategies to recreate synthetic option positions.

These positions offer investors a plethora of ways to obtain their investment goals. Besides synthetic positions, options have many other alternatives. For instance, many investors work with brokers who charge a little margin for shorting stocks. Other traders work with them (brokers) who do not wish to short stocks.

The incapability to do the downside when required limits traders and investors. However, no broker can rule against traders for buying puts in order to 'play the downside.' This is a big benefit for investors.

Options also allow traders to trade the 'third dimension' of the market. Interestingly, they can even trade-in 'no direction,' stock movements, and during volatility. Mostly, stocks do not show 'big' moves; but investors have the edge to trade in stagnation too. Thus, options can only offer multiple alternatives that can give them profit in all types of markets.

Why Options are a Better Choice?

Still, if you want to know why options are a better choice, read this out:

Hedging

The main purpose of inventing options was hedging. It helps to reduce risk. So, take options as your insurance policy. Like you insure your car and home, options can ensure your investment in case of a downfall movement.

Suppose a trader wants to buy something related to tech stocks. But he also wants to limit his loss. The trader can do these easy throughput options, which give him two benefits: minimize risk and maximize profit. Short selling can also reduce loss at the time of a downturn.

Speculation

The ability to predict the future price is speculation, as its name hints. You might think that the price of a stock would go down in a day, based on technical or fundamental analysis. He might sell the stock or sell put after the speculation.

This has got an attraction for many investors to call options because it offers leverage. A call option (out of the money) may cost only some cents of a few dollars compared to the $100 stock's full price.

How does Options Trading work?

When weighing option contracts, it is important to determine the future probabilities. Options get costlier when there is higher predictability in the future. For example, when a stock value rises, the call value also increases. This is crucial to understand the value of options.

A shorter expiry means a lower value of an option as the chances of price rise diminish as the expiry comes near. If a trader purchases an out-of-money 1-month option, while stocks do not move, it losses its value. It is because time is money when it comes to options trading. This wasting con of options is called 'time decay.'

Similarly, if a trader buys an option with a longer expiry; the chances of price movement for that option becomes brighter and brighter as there is enough time for the price to get bigger.

The price also goes up with volatility. When the market is uncertain, the odds get higher. If an asset's volatility goes up, price swings maximize the probability of substantial movements both up and downwards.

Higher price swings also up the chances of an occurring event. It means, the higher the volatility, the greater the options price. Volatility and options trading essentially linked to each other in a way.

On many exchanges, a stock option allows you to buy/sell 100 shares. This is why you should multiply your premium with 100 to get the final amount.

Check out this Example of Investment Table:

	June 1	June 21	Expiry Date
Stock Price	$67	$78	$62
Options Price	$3.15	$8.25	No Value
Contract Value	$315	$825	$0
Paper Loss/Gain	$0	$510	-$315

Most of the time, holders make profits by closing out their positions. Meaning, a holder sells their option; while a writer buys his position back for closing. Not more than 10 percent of the options are executed, and 60 percent are closed (traded out), while 30 expire without having value.

In options, fluctuations can be understood by "time value" (intrinsic and extrinsic value). Their premium is the combination of time value and its intrinsic value. Intrinsic value is the sum above the strike price.

Time value indicates the added value a trader needs to pay above the intrinsic value. This is time value or extrinsic value. Therefore, the option price in the above example can be considered as:

Time Value +	Intrinsic =	Premium
$0.25	$8.00	$8.25

In practical life, Options trade at (some level above) the intrinsic value. It is because the chances of an event's happening can never be absolutely zero – even if it is never in the cards!

Types of Options

There are two major types of options: American and European. The first type can be exercised at any time between the purchase date and expiry. Moreover, Us-based options have a higher premium. The early use feature commends this.

But European options can only be exercised on and near their expiry date. Most of the options on the exchanges belong to the second type.

There is also another type called Exotic Options that are actually a variety of payoff profile from vanilla options. Exotic options are typically meant for professional investors. Other types of options include Binary, Asian, Knock-out, Barrier, and Bermudan Options.

Options Liquidity & Expiry Time

There is another way to categorize options – by the time duration. Short term options expire with 12 months. Long term options have a greater expiry time. They are known as LEAPS or Long-term Equity Anticipation Securities. They are like regular options with typically longer time duration.

Options can also be categorized by their expiry time. Many option sets expire on Fridays, every week, every 30th or 31st of a month, and on a daily basis. There are also quarterly based expiries for ETFs and Index Options.

How to Read Options Table?

It is not possible to do options trading and lack the know-how of reading options tables. Here is how you can read the options table without difficulty.

- You will notice a term "Volume (VLM)" in the table. It indicates the total number of contracts traded in the most recent session.
- You will also hear 'Bid' and 'Ask.' A bid is the most recent price at which the traders wish to purchase an option. While an 'ask' is the most recent price at which the market wishes to sell an option.
- Implied Bid Volatility (IMPL BID VOL) refers to uncertainty in speed and direction of price in the future.
- Delta is the predication or probability. For instance, there are 30 percent chances of expiration of a 30-delta.

- Open Interest (OPTN OP) signifies the grand total of contracts for a specific option. OPTN OP reduces when the open trade closes.
- Gamma (GMM) is called the speed of an option. It can also be called the movement of delta or predication.
- Vega and Theta are two Greek values used in Options trading tables. Vega represents the amount at which an option price is likely to change. Theta represents the degree of value downward change in an option price during a passing day.
- The 'strike price' is a term used for price at which someone buys/sells underlying security if wishes to use options.

3. MAJOR OPTION TRADING CONCEPTS

Options trading is a term that is used in stock exchange the simple definition of options trading is that 'it is the contract between two parties in which the stock option buyer(holder) purchases the right but not the obligation to buy or sell shares of the underlying stock at a predetermined price from/to the option seller (writer) within a fixed period.'

Options offer alternative systems that allow the investor to take advantage of the exchange and trading underlying protections. There are different types of procedures, including different mix options, hidden resources, and different derivatives.

A question will come into your mind that why a person needs options trading at all, options trading is the most efficient method used in the stock exchange and it predates the modern stock exchange by a large margin.

So, one must not think that it is just a scam created by some group of people to manipulate minds to earn money because whenever a common person thinks to invest money in the stock exchange he or she is confused by terms like these, so let us tell you that what options trading is.

History of Option Trading

Some believe that it was the Greeks who gave the idea of option trading. Long before the modern world, humans were trying to decide the prices of different goods, and that's how different methods of trading were introduced into the world.

Let us revise from scratch here...

We will give you a simple example to understand what options trading is but for you to understand we want you to focus on the example with an empty mind, for example, you want to buy stocks for $s 4000 and you go to the broker, but the broker gives you an exciting offer that you can buy stocks for $s 4000 now, or you can give a token of 400 and reserve your write to buy it at $s 4000 after a month, And even if stock increases in value at that time. But the token amount will be non-refundable.

Now you think that it is possible that the stock will increase its price to 4020 at that time and you can even buy it after the increase in price, and since you have only paid 400 so you have the rest of the money to use elsewhere. Now you can wait easily for a month and decide by acknowledging the stock prices after a month that if you want to buy the stock or not.

Now, this is what you all an oversimplification, and this is options trading. In the world of trading, options are used as instruments, just like a musician needs a different instrument to get the perfect song; a broker needs options to make a perfect sale. And its price is mostly derived from stocks.

We assure you that if you read the article to the end, you will perfectly know what option trading is, and we will also tell you different strategies used in options trading.

Risks In Options Trading?

Most strategies that are used by options investors have limited risk but also limited profit, so options trading isn't a method that will make you rich overnight.

Options trading may not suit all types of investors, but they are among the most flexible of investment choices.

Options in investment are most likely used to reduce the risk of a drop in stock prices, but a little risk is involved in every type of investment. Returns are never guaranteed investors look for options to manage risks for ways to limit a potential loss.

Investors may choose to take options because the loss is limited to the price you pay for the token money. And in return, they gain the right to buy or sell stock at there at their desirable price, so options in trading benefit a lot to the investors.

Different Strategies Used In Option Trading

Traders often know very little about strategies used in options trading and jump to trading options, knowing the different strategies may lower the risk of potential loss in the market, and traders may also learn to limit the risk and maximize the return. So with a little effort, traders can learn how to take full advantage of the flexibility and power that stock options can provide.

Stock VS Option

One must think that why is there a need to trade in options when someone can trade simply too this thought confuses many of us so here is the answer

The options contract has an expiration date, depending on what type of options you are using. It may be in weeks, months, or even in years unlike stock, because the stock has no expiration date.

Stocks are usually defined by numbers, but on the other hand, there are no numbers in options.

Options drive their value from something else. That's why they fall into the derivative category, unlike stocks.

Stock owners have their right in the company (dividend or voting)on the other hand options have no right in the company

Some people may find it difficult to understand the method of options though they have even followed it in their other transaction, for example (car insurance or mortgages).

Option Trading Platforms

if a person wants to trade options, he or she must have a brokerage account, and for that, he or she will want to understand what they what before they sign up with a broker. Each platform is unique and has its pros and cons. So a person must learn more about the best options trading platform to determine which one may be the best suited for their needs.

If a person wants to find the best trading platform, he or she must review different brokerages and options trading platforms. A person must consider different factors like competitive pricing, high tech experience, good for a variety of trader needs and styles.

Some of the best options trading platforms for 2020 are:

TD Ameritrade: Best Overall

Tastyworks: Runner-Up

Charles Schwab: Best for Beginners

Webull: Best for No Commissions

Interactive Brokers: Best for Expert Traders

Option Practicing Method

1. Stocks are purchased, and the investor sells call options on the same stock which he has purchased. The number of stock shares you have purchased should match the number of call options you have sold.

2. After buying the stock shares, the investor buys put options to gain equal shares. Married acts as an insurance policy against short-term losses call options with a specific strike price. At the same time, you will sell similar call options at a higher strike price.

3. An investor purchases an option with cash from outside, while simultaneously works an out of the cash call choice for a similar stock.

4. The investor purchases a call option and a put choice simultaneously. The two alternatives ought to have a similar strike cost and expiry date.

5. The Investor purchases the call option out of cash and the put choice simultaneously. They have a similar termination date; however, their strike cost is extraordinary. The expense of the information strike ought to be not exactly the expense of the call strike

Strategies for option trading

Options traders use several strategies to make a profit from this business. The different ways of strategies are used to get profit, which involves using the many alternatives and combinations. The most common strategies are covered calls, iron condors, buying calls, and buying puts. Option trading provides advanced strategies.

Buying calls

Buying calls or long call strategy is used when an investor increasingly buys calls and sets an option on the exact underlying asset with fixed date and price. The investor uses this strategy when they are feeling bullish and confident in an increase in some stock price. In this type, the investor increases the risk as he can face a huge profit or loss, but it's always unknown which way the stock goes.

Buying puts

Usually, the investor uses this strategy when they are bearish on some stock; for example, the investor is confident in a particular stock and had a good understanding of stock but doesn't want to take a huge risk, so he uses short selling strategy.

The put option gets an increase in value when the price of the asset falls. As the market falls, the profit increase in short selling. The risk is not confirmed as the trades return with leverage. But on the off chance that the basic Ascent past the option prices, then the option will expire uselessly.

Covered calls

This strategy provides a small change in the price, the profit is not that big, but the risk it involves is less. The covered call buys 100 shares of stock and then sells one call option per 100 shares. Covered call strategy gives a chance of profit to the investor and also reduce the risk. The share is protected by this call when the price of the stock decreases.

Iron condors

In this strategy, the trader sales a put buys another for a low price and uses them to buy a call then sell the call at a high price after some time. If the stock price is kept somewhere between two puts or calls, then we make a profit. The loss comes with possibilities, one if the price increase suddenly and the other is if the price decrease suddenly, it is spread that causes this condition. This strategy is used by neutral traders or in a neutral place.

Several other strategies are used, which are:

- Broken butterfly
- Iron butterfly
- Jade lizard
- Bear call
- Calendar spread
- Protective put

The Worth of Option Trading

When we buy a bike or car, we want to protect them; the insurance is used for the safety of the car. So just like insurance, the option gives us safety. We invest money and buy shares now we want to protect our investment, for this we use options.

The option provides us good protection of our money. For example:

We bought the 100 shares at the rate of 150 dollars, which Worth 15000. We have invested and now have the risk of a decrease in price. We buy the option to remove risk from our shoulders, and the guy gets paid now assume the risk. We buy the put option for 500 dollars. If the stock increases with the rate of 170, we will get the profit, even buying an option of 500.

But if the stock price decreases with the rate of 130, we still are stable, the loss won't affect us as we have the contract on the option which has the same price. We can sell the shares at the same rate we bought, so in that case, by using the option trade, the chance of loss is very low. It provides a lot of ways to gain profit in trading.

Option Trading VS Stock Trading

An option trading is not stock trading. Well, both of them are trading, but they are quite different. Many people don't even know about the options trading; it's just another type of trading. Few things make the difference between the option trading and stock trading, here is these point.

• In options trading, the value is taken by someone else and had a contract with it. It does not get the values on its own. This is completely different from stock trading. Option trading belongs to the derivative category.

• In stock, the numbers are definite, but an option, the numbers are not definite.

• The options trading use the contract, which has the expiration date, the person has no meaning after the expiry date. The date can be in months or years according to the option there are using. Stock trading has no expiration dates.

• In options trading, the owner has no right in the company. They have no affair of any kind related to the company. In stock share, they had the rights to the company.

Risk in Option Trading

The risk involves in option is not as much as people think. Trading does involve risk. Its procedures work along with the risk. In option, the risk can contain only in few things.

• The options trading use many strategies with these strategies. Each has its own risk. The few options work on the spontaneous increase and decrease process. This sometimes gives a big loss to the investor.

• The option involves a lot of complexity. This trading is bot difficult to understand. The strategies its self are complex. Those who are a beginner in option do not understand it well and invest the money with the little knowledge which results in a loss.

• The other problem with the options trading is that it has the expiration date, which can cause you all you invest if the contract expires. This is one big factor in this trading.

Option Account

For option trade, you need an options account. Before you make an account, you need to fill the agreement with your broker. The broker will know your investment and your trade. He will generate the strategy according to the level of trading you want. The broker will guide you about options trading and its policies.

What Is An Option Account?

The account that is used to access the option trade is an options account. The broker gives access to the user for an options account. For all the trading, the brokerage account is used; it does the selling and buying. After giving all details, you will be able to open the account.

The broker tells the two type of account which you want to open, the real money and demo money account. After all the procedures, your account will ready for trading.

The Right Broker

Before choosing your broker, you check in on him. Always choose the one with an authentic source. The information you provide him should be protected. Always check the payment and its cost. Aim for the right option.

The Best Broker

- Schwab Brokerage ($0.65 per options contract)
- E-trade ($0.65 per options contract)
- Ally Invest ($0.5 per contract traded)
- TD Ameritrade ($0.65 fee per contract)

Best platforms

Options trading is a high-level risk. It needs to be protected from fraud. When selecting the platform, you must select the best one. There are many best platforms available in the market; there has a good reputation, such as.

- Charles Schwab, this platform is best for the beginner. If you are a beginner, you should choose this platform. This platform gives more understanding to users.

- TD Ameritrade is the best platform dor the options trading in the world. The cost is low and no account minimum requirements

- Tastyworks provide trading access to different devices. It allows PC, laptops, and mobile phones. It is one of the most high-tech platforms.

Webull platform gives no commission

Options trading is not meant for beginners who have zero ideas about the market. So if you are just starting your journey with the stock market, you may have to spend some time learning the basic concepts of options trading.

When we talk about stocks, it's all about investment and turning that investment into profit. So it requires strong knowledge and experience to make some big profits and avoid loss.

4. OPTIONS TRADING MYTHS AND MISCONCEPTIONS

There are many myths and misconceptions related to the term "Options Trading" not only in the stock market but also for the general public. Options trading is known to be risky; according to Mike Bellafiore, the Co-Founder of CMB trading, "Trading is a sport of survival, reinvention, and perseverance, even for the successful trader."

Indeed, in the stock market or business, there is no such thing as assurance; there is always a risk involved with putting your money into something. The stock market or business is always about numbers and good strategies. If your strategies and numbers are right, you are in it for the long haul; otherwise, you will end up with nothing.

The winner of U.S. Investing Championship in 1984 Martin S. Schwartz says,

"A lot of people get so enmeshed in the markets that they lose their perspective. Working longer does not necessarily equate with working smarter. In fact, sometimes it's the other way around." in a trading business, you can use your shortcomings or failures for your future benefits as well; according to Brett Steenbarger, an active trader and a Ph.D. scholar, "we will never be perfect as traders. That's what keeps us ever-learning, ever-growing. Our main challenge is to use our shortcomings as inspirations, fueling continuous improvement."

There are many myths and misconceptions about trading.

Misconception #1 Trading and Gambling are same

The first and the most common one is trading and gambling are the two sides of the same coin. In trading, a trader goes through all the present, past data, and numbers whether gambling is a game of available odds.

Trading is about technical analysis you look into the details, risks, profit, gain, and the market, whereas gambling is based on fundamental values. You put in your money in what you might think will happen. Also, gambling is an addiction, illegal, and also very toxic for your mental health and behavior.

Misconception #2 Should only invest in Call and Put Option

Options are the type of contract that allows the buyer to purchase or sell the underlying asset. To simplify it, the trader purchases a call option if he is expecting the demand of the underlying asset to rise within a certain deadline, and the trader opts for a put option if he is expecting the demand of the underlying asset to fall within a certain time period.

It is a misconception about the call and put option that it is the only profitable way of trading options, but in reality, the buying of calls and puts is highly risky in trading because you can never be sure about the demand of the underlying asset for that you need the proper analysis of the direction it is moving, its time frame and size of the move. You can analyze the size and the direction right, but if your options have expired before the move happens, then you may lose money.

Misconception #3 Option selling is more profitable

Option selling is basically giving someone the right, but not the obligation, to make you purchase 100 shares of a stock at a strike price before the expiration date. In simpler terms, they are basically paying to increase their flexibility, and you pay to decrease your flexibility. So when you are selling options, you are not only using the money in your brokerage, but you are also in debt. Option selling can be profitable if you play right by the rules, but there is also high risk involved in it.

Misconception #4 Put Option expire worthlessly

Option expiring worthless is when options expire from your trading account and cease to exist. There are a lot of misconceptions about 90 percent of the option expiring, but according to the report by The Chicago Board Options Exchange (CBOE), approximately, only 30% of the options expire worthlessly. 60% of the option positions are closed before their expiration, and 10% of the options are exercised.

Secondly, options expiring worthless, only work against the option buyers, but option writers still get their profit if the put option has expired.

Misconception #5 Option trading is a zero-sum

This is one of the oldest myths about option trading. It says that if a buyer wins, then the seller has to lose. But no, that is not true at all!

Options are given to manage the risk. They do not give you anything of value other than the choice to buy or sell assets. When you use options to hedge your risk, you are transferring your risk to someone else who is willing to hold on to it. So the options trading is not a zero-sum game.

Misconception #6 Options trading is easy

There is another misconception about options trading that people assume it is easy. According to the Charles Faulkner trader and an author he says "After years of studying traders, the best predictor of success is simply whether the person is improving with time and experience" you need years of experience, learning the market and its resources completely and strategies then you can be a successful trader.

Trading is rarely about "luck" its all about good hand-on knowledge. People do not mostly have an in-depth knowledge of the options trading or stock market. It is more than just investing the money. All the experts in trading business have years of experience and knowledge, and they even use their failures as a weapon for their future success.

Misconception #7 Trading in Tax-deferred account

There is a common misconception about using traditional or IRA accounts for the trading option because they both will ease up the tax advantage, and It could be a perfect retirement plan, but there are certain limits to it. You can only invest to a certain limit through your tax-deferred account. You cannot use the money before retirement. After five years, you are only able to withdraw the income.

5. TOP OPTIONS TRADING STRATEGIES

The options trading utilizes a few strategies for financial specialists to benefit from trading. The various methods of strategies are utilized to get profit, which includes utilizing the numerous other options and combinations.

The alternative exchanging gives advance techniques. These systems help financial specialists to increase the most extreme benefits. The top strategy is used for different levels of trading. Many popular trading strategies are used in the market. These strategies are well known in trading and have numbers of users. The following are the top option trading strategies.

Buying calls

Purchasing calls or long call methodology is utilized when a financial specialist progressively purchases calls and sets a choice on the specific hidden resource with fixed date and cost. The investor expects more leverage than just owning the stock. The financial specialist uses this procedure when they are feeling bullish and certain about increment at some stock cost. The confidence of the investor prepares them to pick this option strategy.

In this sort, the speculators increment the hazard as he can confront the gigantic benefit or loss, but it's consistently obscure what direction the stock goes. If the stock goes up, the investor will get the profit, and if the shares price decrease, then the investor will face a big loss. Even the most experienced traders face loss at some point, but that does not mean it will only give loss.

The profit in it usually covers the loss of investors. For example, If the investor wants to buy a developing house, then he will purchase the buy call option by doing this he can pay the same price according to the contract as the cost of a house is 200,000 now as when the development will be complete, the cost of the house will be increased.

Suppose the price of the house incredibly increased after 2,3 years, and now the house is worth 400,000. The investor will pay the same amount, although its price in the market is double because of the option he can pay the same amount of 200,000 as written on the contract. The only thing the investor will be worried about is the expiration date.

Buying puts

In this options trading strategy, the investor has the legal right to sell the shares at the given price. The date is also fixed at a certain time. The buying puts give more authority to the investor.

Normally, the financial specialist utilizes this strategy when they are bearish on some stock; for the model, the speculator is positive about the specific stock and had great comprehension of stock yet wouldn't like to face an immense challenge, so he utilizes short selling procedure.

The put choice gets increment in esteem when the cost of benefit falls. As the market falls, the benefit increment by short selling. The chance isn't affirmed as the trade return with leverage. But if the fundamental Ascent past the choice value, then the alternative will terminate pointlessly.

Mostly the traders are sure that the market will fall. They purchase the share to sell it at a certain time as they have the right to do so, the values of share increase when the stock moves towards the other direction. It is a simple way to gain profit.

If you want the insurance on your shares in stock, you can buy a put option. If the investor has a share of 500 dollars, and he realized the market would lose the value. They can sell there share at a reduced price of about 475 dollars. The loss is reduced in this way.

Covered call

This strategy provides a small change in the price, the profit is not that big, but the risk it involves is less. The covered call buys 100 shares of stock and then sale one call option per 100 shares. Covered call strategy gives a chance of profit to the investor and also reduce the risk.

The share is protected by this call when the price of the stock decreases. In this strategy, the seller of the call option possesses the related amount of underlying instrument. In the covered call option, you can buy stock and sell the call option on Out of money(OTM).

The term buy-write is referred to when the call been sold at the same time with the purchase of stock. We get a small amount for call sales when we pay for stock shares. We have to sell calls to generate income in it. This option needs direct investment and calls to sell.

The investor uses this option strategy when they think the price will not further increase. We have to hold a long position. The chance of profit is low as the increase in price is not expected.

Suppose, the stock was trading at $200 on May 20th, 2014; The Leg 1 Buy 100 portions of the stock for $ 200 and Leg 2: Sell the 206 strikes June 26th, 2014 Call for $7.30, Lot size – 100 offers

The sum paid to take these two positions approaches - the Stock cost paid less call premium got, for example, $. 20,000 (Stock buy) – $ 730 (Premium got) = $ 19,270

If the stock value ascends over the call strike of 206, it will be worked out, and the stock will be sold. In any case, the methodology will make a benefit since you are secured by the stock you own.

State, the stock cost at termination is $ 210.

In the event that the stock falls beneath the underlying stock price tag, your long position is at a misfortune. However, you have some pad from the call premium got by selling the call.

State, the stock falls and is at $ 190 on the lapse

Iron condors

In this strategy, the trader sales a put buys another for a low price and uses them to buy a call then sell the call at a high price after some time. If the stock price is kept somewhere between two puts or calls, then we make a profit.

The loss comes with possibilities, one if the price increase suddenly and the other is if the price decrease suddenly, it is spread that causes this condition. This strategy is used by neutral traders or in a neutral place. This is a simple options strategy.

The iron condors option does not require a big investment to start a trade; you can start the trade with a minimum amount. The investor relies on the stock to stay at some particular point. It is a small strategy that involves risk, but the investor invests in a small amount to maintain the risk.

Consider the stock is trading at the cost of $120, executing an Iron Condor trading procedure we will: Sell $100 Strike Put for $3.0 Sell $140 Strike Call for $3.0

With an expectation that the cost will stay inside these two strike costs that we booked so, we make a benefit. In any case, because of the danger of boundless misfortune, we would ensure our situations by Buy Strike Put for $90 Buy Strike $160 Call for $ 2.

Bear calls

This option works on the procedure of sale and buy. The investor sells the call option and then purchases the calls at a high strike rate. This option uses the investment of the trader to get the profit income. The procedure works on limited levels. It uses two legs. These work on a 1:1 ratio to make the net credit.

Even though this is not a Bearish Strategy, it is actualized when one is bullish. It is generally set up for a 'net credit,' and the expense of buying call choices is financed by selling an 'in the cash' call choice. For this Options Trading Strategy, one must guarantee the Call alternatives have a place with a similar expiry, the equivalent hidden resource, and the proportion is kept up.

It, for the most part, ensures the drawback of a Call sold by safeguarding it, for example, by purchasing a Call of a higher strike cost. It is fundamental, however, that you execute the system just when you are persuaded that the market would be moving essentially higher.

The investor is expecting a small decrease in the stock. They sell the calls and then purchase the calls at high strike. The option works better when the volatility is high. The expiration date is good enough to handle things. The traders don't waste the expiry date, as it is important for the trading. The investor uses the long term to execute the process.

If the market is expecting the rise in stock, then the traders sell the one strike call and then buy another at the higher strike. The investor gets the profit by the amount of cost.

If the stock is expecting a sudden rise, then they sales the call and then buy the new ones which they even buy at a high rate, but instead of loss they gain profit, and then they buy more calls.

Jade lizard

In this options trading strategy, the traders sell short calls and put, and the underlying assets should not move. The cost collect in the results is great. All the options have the same expiration date. It minimizes the risk and maximizes the reward. Trading options maximize the risk in one direction.

The jade lizards option are a sort of Options Trading Strategy which is rehearsed by Traders to pick up benefit from their exchanges

If there should arise an occurrence of Straddles and Strangles, Lizards diminish the upside hazard. They are most valuable when basic stays or floats toward the strike. High benefits are created in high IV and non-bearish situations. This neutral strategy involves short calls and short put spread. It is a slow strategy; it does not increase suddenly. It uses the call cost and puts the cost at high volatility.

Let's suppose that the investor accepts this trade is a drawback chance. In the event that ABC stock moves above £25 per share, the financial specialist would lose $£1 on the call spread, yet gains £1.10 from the premium gathered for a net addition of £0.10.

The investor benefits from the exchange, except if the cost of ABC moves underneath the strike cost of the bare put by more than the top-notch that is gathered. In this model, the stock cost would need to dip under £18.90.

Collar option

It is similar to the covered call but has extra protective puts to protect the value of security between 2 bounds. The Collar Options Trading Strategy can be built by holding portions of the hidden all the while and purchasing put-call alternatives and selling call choices against the held offers.

One can support the expected drawback in the offers by purchasing the fundamental and, at the same time, purchasing a put alternative beneath the current cost and selling a call choice over the current cost. Buy one put option than lower the limit for protection; sell the call option at the upper limit.

Both must have the same expiration date and the quantity. The call and put options are out of money. The underlying assets price expired at a strike price of the short call option. The instability is surprising when the market is unstable at the point when the cost of an alternative ascent, there is a likelihood that the cost may fall and you may miss out on the benefit.

In such a case, the advantage should be secured. The option protects the losses a lot and decreases the chances of all loss, but with all the protection, sometimes it reduces the profit.

Let us guess that stock value rises to Rs 50In this case; the trader would have understood the estimation of his stock holding rise to (100*50) = Rs 5000.

As he is the seller of the Call option, he anticipated that the cost of the fundamentals should fall. In any case, its cost has, in certainty, risen. The Call option purchaser will practice his privilege and will purchase the Call alternative at the strike cost of 48, which is lower than the cost of the fundamental that is 50. So the option seller got (48*100) = Rs 4800 by selling the Call option.

For a Put alternative purchaser, an option is in the cash if the strike cost is higher than the cost of the hidden. For this situation, as the strike cost of 43 is not exactly the CMP of the hidden, which is 50, and along these lines, the option is rendered useless for him.

Net benefit from the exchange = Rs 5000 – Rs 4800+500 - 300 = 400

Diagonal spread

The diagonal spread option strategy uses many strikes and months. It works with the combined bits of a long call spread and a short call spread. Diagonal spread moves diagonally and also the names.

The option is presented in different rows and columns. In this options trading strategy, the short terms are sold, and long terms are bought. A transient shortcoming or Strength that you think would go up or go down once more, at that point, to the advantage of it.

The system is controlled on the short-side for risk, and if the market plays smoothly, it can become open-finished on the long side.

At the point when executed for cash, it permits edge necessities to be met. The investment is at high risk when it works quickly in our way. The diagonal spread has its setup, which we have to follow.

- The equal number of options is required.

- The options must have the exact underlying security.

- The options in the diagonal spread should have the same class.

- The different expiry dates are used.

- The two different strike prices.

In the diagonal spread, the bullish long call diagonal spread purchases the option with the lower strike rate and longer expiry date then sells the short date option with high strike rates.

Butterfly

The broken wing butterfly option is a bit similar to the butterfly trading strategy, but In this trading strategy, the calls and puts are much similar to directional strategy rather than the butterfly strategy.

Its sides have a different level of risk; the risk is different on each side. Usually, the profit occurs if the underlying expires at the short strike price. The broken wing butterfly option provides more profit than the butterfly option.

Futuresmag merits the credit for begetting the "Broken Wing Butterfly," an amazing option in contrast to the Butterfly, where the objective is starting an exchange at zero expense.

It is an amazing options trading which expands on the positive attributes of a Butterfly Spread. Dissimilar to the Long Butterfly, where one needs to pay another charge, Broken Wing Butterfly Strategy is a net credit procedure, frequently rehearsed to build the likelihood of benefit.

Broken Wing Butterfly Strategy is equivalent to a Butterfly in which the sold spread is regularly more extensive spread than the bought spread. It has the similarity of long butterfly spread having the same strikes that are not much different from the short strike. It works when the option has all the puts or all the calls.

For example, the stock is trading at Rs100. You buy one 120 calls on ABC, you sell two 105 calls in ABC and purchase one 100 calls in ABC, So you get the net credit of Rs. 10.

6. TOP QUALITIES OF A SUCCESSFUL OPTIONS TRADER

'The key to trading success is emotional discipline. If intelligence were the key, there would be a lot more people making trading money' – Victor Sperandeo

To be an options trader, certain qualities are required that are not at all difficult to achieve. To develop those qualities, you have to know about the options trading.

Options Trading

In options trading, the buyer has the right, when he wants to buy (the case of a call) and when he wants to sell (the case of a put) but he is not bound to buy or sell the certain asset at a specific price, as the name 'Options' suggest. The trader is also not bound to trade in some specific time. He has the total choice of what and when he wants to trade.

Why people tend to go for options trading?

Options can provide better income than any other job. It is not much different than the stock exchange. It is just like your own business; all you have to do is predict where the market and stock rates are going. You have to take a risk, but the income will be higher than you have thought. The end results can give a shock as market rates keep on changing every minute.

Top Qualities of a Successful Options Trader

Just like in any other business, there is a huge risk of loss. Every other person cannot be a good businessman. Many people have weak patience level, they lose their heart, and on failure, they leave the business or sell at a low price without giving another try.

The one who buys that at a low price takes it to another level. Similarly, everyone cannot be a good trader. Being a successful trader demands certain qualities. If you achieve those qualities, nothing can stop you from becoming one of the most successful options traders.

1. Control on emotions
2. Record keeping
3. Finding the right strategy for you
4. Consistency
5. Learning from failures
6. News interpretation
7. Being yourself
8. Patience
9. Flexibility
10. Risk management

These are a few qualities to make you a successful trader in options trading, and a positive attitude towards these skills can make you a professional options trader. Let's dig a bit more into these qualities to polish your personality a little more.

Control on Emotions

Mixing your emotions with your business can take you towards destruction. You have to manage your social life along with the real-life without tangling them with each other. You must be able to manage the happening in real life and happenings in the business. You must have total control over your mind and hold your nerves while doing the business.

Records Management

If you keep a record of whatever you do, next time you will be able to avoid the mistake you have made previously, and you will be able to see where you have gone wrong.

This habit will provide you information on your wealth to improving your odds of success. By keeping the records, you will be able to make up your previous losses. Records will also help you keep track of profit/losses for tax purposes, if applicable.

A Good Planner

Everyone has their own strategy (like the way of doing things). Some people tend to go for short sales and make multiple sales in a day. Others hit their luck after a long time and make a large amount by a single sale.

Even if they perform a single sale in a week, they can earn more than the one who makes many sales in a day. Once you find the right strategy for yourself, you have to stick with that strategy. It is crucial which strategy you are choosing for yourself. It is because in options trading, the right strategy and technique to trade will take you to the top, and the wrong will do the opposite.

Consistency

Nothing other than small chunks can be earned without consistency. You have to give a lot to achieve a lot. In the case of options trading, you have to invest your time to achieve experience. The more experience you get, the more you learn.

Like you learn when and where to put your money; and when to draw it out. Many people get back when they see smaller earnings, not knowing that smaller steps lead towards greater steps.

Learning from Failures

Just as most businessmen lose their money, similarly, every trader also faces losses. This is just part of the game! But a successful trader doesn't give up on his loss and try to avoid loss in the future from the experience he gained from his previous loss.

Then a time comes when he has learned every possible reason leading to his loss. In the future, he can cover up his previous losses by avoiding the same mistake.

News Interpretation

The traders must be able to interpret the news. If you are good at interpreting the news, you will have the exact knowledge to predict which is the product will give profit and when. If you can predict the future, you'll be able to raise your income by investing in a certain product.

You'll also be able to predict when to buy or sell the product to maximize your profit. Some news is just the hype; you have to be able to differentiate between the real news and the hype.

Do not Follow What Others are Doing

Everyone has their thinking. But once you come to the trade business, do not rely completely on others' strategies. In order to be a successful trader, you don't have to do what everyone else is doing. You have to be limitless and be yourself. You may come out of your comfort zone, but following your own passion will be the key to success. Your willingness to take risks will benefit you in being yourself.

Patience

Being a successful options trader demands a lot of patience. You have to be able to wait until; it's the right time to perform the action. It means, if you have to put your money into something, you have to wait until you think; it is the lowest price for a certain product. Similarly, while selling, you have to be patient until it reaches the highest amount of profits.

If you are not patient while trading; a huge loss may be on your way!

Flexibility

The rates of market changes every day; you have to be able to learn the changing dimensions of the market. You have to learn about the changing trends of the market and adopt newer strategies.

You have to be well aware of the relevant news and always believe yourself as a learner. You have to accept the losses as loss in any field of work is inevitable. You have to accept wherever the market is going, whether it suits you or not.

Risk Management

In options, you are playing in millions, so there is a huge risk. You have to manage how much risk you can bear at a certain time. Being limitless does not mean you have to forget about what you are risking while putting your money. If you allot a certain capital to an investment, you may be able to avoid a higher risk of loss but, the greater the risk, the greater will be the gains or losses.

Conclusion

If you have these certain skills or qualities, one day, you will be the most successful trader of the options trading. Just be patient and have consistency in your work. The doors of success will keep opening for you. The most important thing is believing in yourself; if you take larger risks and have belief in yourself, there is nothing you cannot do.

7. HOW TO SELECT THE RIGHT OPTION FOR A MAJOR GAIN

Starting from simple purchases to more complicated spreads like butterflies, options have a plethora of strategies. Moreover, they are available for a bigger range of currencies, stocks and commodities, futures contracts, and exchange-traded funds.

Often, there are hundreds of expiries and strike prices for each option. This poses a challenge for the novices to select the best option out of many. Here is how you can do that like a pro.

Look for the Right Option

Imagine, you already have an asset in mind that you wish to trade on, like a commodity. You picked it from stock screener through your insight and the insight of others (e.g. research). Regardless of the selection technique, after identifying your asset for trading, you need to follow these steps to achieve your goal.

- Frame your purpose of investment
- Determine your payoff
- Analyze volatility
- Recognize events

- Make a Strategy
- Launch parameters of options

These steps follow a logical process, which makes it easy to select the right option to trade on. Let us breakdown what these steps reveal.

Frame your Purpose

The base of getting into the trading business is finding the purpose of investment. Why do you want to start options trading? What is the purpose behind this? Do you want to make real money, or is it just a side-business? Ask yourself these questions. Make a notebook and write all the answers that you have.

Now you might be thinking, why so? It is because you need to be clear on this point. Using options to make real money is very different as compared to purchasing them for speculating or hedging.

This is your first step, and it will form the foundation for other steps. So, buckle up!

Trader's Payoff

In the second step, determine your risk and reward payoff. This should be dependent upon your appetite or tolerance for risk. Know your type – like if you are one of the conservative traders, using aggressive strategies for options trading might not be suitable for you. These strategies include purchasing deep out-of-money options in large quantities or writing puts etcetera.

Each strategy has a well-made risk and reward profile. You have got to keep an eye on it. And do not forget to assess your payoff at the end of the day!

Analyze Volatility

It is one of the most crucial steps in options trading. You have got to analyze implied volatility for sure. Compare it to the history of options stock volatility, plus the volatility level in the market.

This allows you to know about the thinking of other traders. Whether they expect the stocks to move fast or up in the future or not, if there is high volatility, there will be a higher premium too. In this case, options writing will be more suitable for you.

A lower rate of implied volatility means there will be lower premium – good for the purchase of options (if you think that the stocks will move more and so their value will increase as well).

Recognize Events

There are two main types of events: stock-specific and market-wide. Stock specific events include types like spin-offs, product launches, and earnings reports, etcetera. Market-wide events, on the other hand, are those that have a huge role in broad markets like economic data releases and Federal Reserve Announcements.

It is important that you know and recognizes each event type. Since they have a huge impact on implied volatility and, thus, can have a great impact on the price when it occurs. Recognizing events before they can help traders to make a bigger profit, determine the right time and the appropriate expiration date for your trade.

Make Your Strategy

The first four steps allow you to see clearly the way to your options trading business. Now you are in a good position to devise your own plan after knowing the events, implied volatility, risk, and reward pay off and your investment goal.

Suppose a conservative trader with a good portfolio wishes to earn premium within some months. He should then use the covered call "writing" technique to achieve his goal. While an aggressive investor who foresees market decline within some months should purchase puts on main stocks so on.

Launch Parameters

After the fifth step is clear on your mind, try to launch parameters. For instance, you should establish the expiration time, option delta, and strike price, etcetera. Let us say a trader wants to buy the longest expiration date call. But he also wants to pay a low premium on it. In this case, the out-of-the-money call is the most appropriate for him. But for a high delta call, focus on in-the-money option.

In short, follow the given steps to make a good profit and establish yourself as a professional options trader in the market. Determine your objective of investment, analyze your risk and reward, assess volatility, think about the happenings, make your strategy, and then tailor your options parameters.

How to make money with Options Trading

An Option trader earns money by buying or selling or by being an option writer.

With options trading, you do not only buy or own stock in a company, but you are also in a position to sell that stock in the future. If you know the right strategies, you can earn above 100,815$ through options trading. Learning the right strategies, knowledge about risks, learning the market, multiplying the profit, and building wealth will help you make more money with options trading.

Earning Money with options trading in 2020

We have enlisted some special Options Trading techniques that could help you understand and earn money better through Options Trading.

Recap

Before really getting into the business, you need to recap what options trading really is, what its terms are, and how it's done with minimum risks involved. In simple terms, options trading is buying and selling options contracts.

Options trading does not allow you to vote or receive dividends or anything else a (partial) owner of the company can do. It is just a contract between you and some other party that grants you the right to purchase (i.e., "call option") or sells (i.e., "put option") stock of a company at a certain price.

It is one of the most basic 'leveraging' tools available to investors who are looking to increase their potential profit by accepting the increase in risk that always comes attached to it.

There are some essential key terms that are normally used in Options Trading:

Stock

A stock option is a contract between the company and the stock option buyer to buy or sell 100 shares of the company at a determined amount within a certain time period.

Expiration

In options trading, there is a contract involved, and each contract has an expiration date. You can buy or sell your options before the expiration date, but once it crosses the expiration date, the contract has no value to it. In that case, only an option writer can earn.

Strike Price

A strike price is a price at which the commodity or asset is to be bought or sold when the option is exercised. For example, if the strike price is XYZ dollars for a call option, then you could exercise your contract by purchasing the identified stock at the strike price.

Premium

Options Premium is the price to be paid by the party who is purchasing the right buy/the right to sell, to the party that is selling the right to buy/the right to sell, as a premium to enter into a contract for the risk of the option being exercised if the contract is in the money, that the writer (seller) of option is bearing while entering into the option contract. It depends on the strike price, the volatility of the underlying, and expiration date.

Call and Put Option

In options trading, there is a call and Put option A call is when you buy or purchase a stock and put is when you sell a stock. You can buy or sell a stock before the expiration date.

Underlying Asset

The underlying asset is reference security (stock, bond, futures contract, etc.) on which the price of derivative security like an option is based. For example, options are derivative instruments, meaning that their prices are derived from the price of another security. More specifically, options prices are derived from the price of an underlying stock.

Option Style

An option contract is made up of two different styles; American style or European style. Options can be practiced in a particular way, and both styles allow you to practice them differently. American style options can be used any time before expiration, whereas European style options can only be used on expiration dates itself.

Contract Multiplier

The contract multiplier states the quantity of the underlying asset that needs to be delivered in the event the option is exercised. For stock options, each contract covers 100 shares.

Relative Value

Selling a commodity at a higher price than the buying price and purchasing at a lower price than the market or what you sold it as.

Making Money with Options Trading in 2020

Option traders use different strategies to evaluate the trade. A list of tools is included in the process of evaluation.

The list might include; analysis, history, statistics, stability, debt, dividends, etc.

With a little reading, a trader can easily minimize his risk of losing his investment. Here are the top 10 strategies of how to make money through options trading:

Naked Call

A naked call is an options strategy in which an investor sells (a call option) without the security of owning the underlying stock.

Covered Put

A covered option is a strategy where the stock is bought or owned, and an option is sold. The underlying stock is bought, and simultaneously writes–or sells–a call option on those same shares. The Covered Put also has a higher profit in case the stock moves down to the strike price of the short puts.

For example, an investor uses his call option (buys) on a stock that represents 100 shares of stock per call option. For every 100 shares of stock that the investor purchases, they will sell one call option against it. This strategy is referred to as a covered call because, in the event that a stock price increases rapidly, this investor's short call is covered by the long stock position.

The formula for calculating maximum profit is:

Max Profit = Premium Received - Commissions Paid

Max Profit Achieved When Price of Underlying <= Strike Price of Short Put

Making most out of options

Options are like a business; not everyone can achieve high wages or income. To be a successful businessman, you need a certain type of mindset, few skills, and a little capital. While discussing how to make money through options, we don't have to only look onto physical strategies but also mental and indirect strategies.

Indirect Strategies:

Record keeping

Keeping proper records of your progress is really helpful for a successful practical life as well as for business. In options, you can track your progress, the weaknesses, and the reasons for these weaknesses. It will help you to learn from your mistakes and avoid them in the future.

Stay aware

Technology keeps on developing every day; each day, we see new innovation. To walk with others and avoid staying behind them, you must have access to the latest news and updates about technology and stay ready for what is coming next.

Stay updated

To be a successful options trader, you have to be updated on what is going on in the stock market and how and when prices are going to change. This way you will be able to predict the prices of the market and plan your move accordingly to avoid losses

Mental strategies:

Managing the risk

It is a famous saying, "Cut your coat according to the cloth." Applying this on options, you have to agree that don't put all your money into one product. Only invest as much amount for which you can bear the risk.

Managing time

No one can force you to put or call the money in a certain product until you yourself want to do so. Look for the perfect time to do so, invest only when you know it is a perfect time. The most important thing is patience. But keep track of the expiration date.

Separate practical and business life

To make progress as an options trader, never mix up your emotions with your business. If you are going through something bad in real life and getting frustrated, mind taking a break. A fresh mind can think well than the mind busy in solving other issues. Options trading is the game of the mind, so take a break and come back when you are relaxed.

These are the few physical, mental, and indirect strategies that we have discussed above. Hope, this will take you to the heights of success and make most out of options.

8. IMPORTANT TIPS & TRICKS ABOUT OPTIONS TRADING

An option trading is a part of trading that allows you to trade your market expectations while also control the risk that you are going to participate in this trading with. Now, if you get a better a clearer idea of how to rightly perform options trading, there are no limitations to it. This means that you can trade various strategies and seek profit in all sorts of market conditions.

However, this options trading doesn't mean that you have to trade the strategies of your complex trading options to seek profit from them. Instead, you can spend your money more effectively to gain profit by simply replacing your regular trading positions with the help of options.

A Little Insight:

With the start of 2020, the options trading activity has achieved a drastic increase. Now, if we calculate the increase in the options contracts in this year up until now, an estimation of a 53% increase has been calculated – in comparison to that of the same time last year. Hence, there can certainly not be a better time to head onto the trading options activity – if you're thinking about it.

However, understanding the trading options strategies and how it can be performed properly is very important. Therefore, even if you're a pro in trading, it's important to know the major and important tips regarding options trading. Now, these strategies and tips may change according to the conditions and criteria of the market.

But to give you a consistent answer of how you can firmly perform options trading, we'll discuss some tips below that might just do the trick. So without further ado, let's go ahead and discover some such tips!

Follow a Well Defined Exit Plan

Controlling your emotions while trading options can be crucial in terms of helping you achieve great profits. This crucial step can be defined by simply having a plan to work and always sticking to it. This way, you are well aware of the outcome you desire when following that plan, and you can surely achieve it. So no matter how much your emotions force you to change your mind and forget our plan while you're on it, make sure you don't!

Now when you make a well-defined plan, you can't miss on the exit planning here too. This exit plan doesn't mean that you are supposed to minimize your loss in terms of facing the downside of options trading. But instead, having a well-defined exit plan and a downside exit plan in advance can help you get out of the trade at the right time – even if the trade is going right according to your plan.

This is very important because options trading is an activity that faces a decay in the rates when the expiration date starts coming closer.

Educate Yourself

Trading options can be a complex activity in comparison to simply buying and selling stocks. And if you don't understand this activity well, there are chances that you might not be able to get anywhere in it. However, if you keep seeking knowledge and experience in this, you'll be better aware of how you can invest here and gain profit.

Now to get started in this, you need to have a proper assessment of your investment plan. This assessment can include your individual goals, the risk constraints, the time horizon, tax constraints, and the liquidity needs you have.

Don't Double Up for Past Losses

If you are thinking of doubling on an options strategy just because you want to cover your past loss, then you're surely not going to get far with this. A simple reason for that is that options in options trading are simply derivatives, and their prices properties aren't the same as the underlying stock holds them.

Therefore, even if it sometimes makes sense to double up just so that you can catch up on the loss you faced earlier (and because you follow this in the stocks), it doesn't mean that it will also serve you with profit when you're in the options galaxy.

Hence, instead of enhancing your risk, you should simply step back and close the trade. This way, you can cut more of your losses that might further come in the same trade, and simply go for a different opportunity. As a result, instead of digging deeper into the specific options category, you will be accepting your loss and saving yourself from a bigger downfall.

Manage Your Risk

Now the most important aspect here is the risk of the options trading. So when you go for options trading, you must understand how much risk you can take. Whether you're a beginner or someone who has been in the options trading for a while, having a certain risk assessment that you can handle is very important.

Once you have that, you can look into the different methods that can help you manage your risks. Now to manage the risks, you can go for different options throughout the life of the options contract – to manage the risks. These different options include:

Closing a Trade: this mainly refers to taking an offsetting position in the trade. So if you have purchased a call option in trading options, you can simply set the call option and close the trade for managing the risk on time.

Allowing an Option to Expire

This can be possible when a contract in trading options has reached its expiration date without being worked on. Here, you can also purchase or sell a call or put, according to the contract.

Roll out an Option

This is mainly the process of managing risk by simply closing an option that is near to the expiration date, and then simultaneously investing in a similar category of trade that has a distant expiration date.

Assignment

Lastly, another strategy of managing the risks in trading options is to simply go for an assignment. This is possible when you sell an option by simply receiving or delivering the shares that lie under the stock of that option.

Finally

Now trading options are quite a familiar trading aspect for many, but most of the new traders aren't very familiar with it. However, achieving great profits and success in trading options is something anyone can achieve. Only if you educate yourself in this, gain some experience, and righty follow efficient tips and tricks (as mentioned above) – you are sure to go far in trading options.

9. IMPORTANT FAQS OF OPTIONS TRADING

We tried to include all the basic and important frequently asked questions regarding options trading. Hope they help you understand the options trading better and if not. You can post your inquiries in the comment section.

Is there any definition of options?

Options are derivatives that are supported on the value of underlying securities such as stocks.

Options are putting down your money for the right to buy a stock at a specific price before its expiration date. There are two types of options; options buy or sell.

When an investor takes part in options, s/he is either buying or selling an options contract and is making a bet that either the underlying share will rise in price or fall in price before the expiration date.

How to gain maximum profit in options trading?

According to Allen Everhart, the best way to maximize profit in options trading is to just keep it simple. In his words, "I have come to appreciate buying deep-in-the-money/deep-in-time call options despite the disparagement this strategy gets."

Purchase a 70 delta call if you think the market is going higher - or put if you think the market is falling. You will not need to worry much about theta decay (there's a little, but not much) and you'll profit 80% of a $1 move on the stock or ETF at a much lower cost than an equivalent number of shares of stock, and there's no risk of being randomly exercised and having the stock (long or short) suddenly appear in your account the next morning!

When you have 200 short option positions on, and a dozen of them get randomly exercised overnight, you will appreciate the 'simple' approach to options trading.

What happens in a case when options contract expires?

In case if the contract reaches its expiration date and you have not yet exercised your right to options, then you will lose your right and premium. The contract becomes invalid.

The only person who will profit from this is the writer of the contract.

What is the difference between strike price and stock price?

A strike price is a price at which the owner of an option can execute the contract, whereas; a stock price is the last transaction price of at least a single share of an underlying.

What is naked call?

It's a strategy in which an investor writes a call option without having a position in the underlying stock itself. To set up a naked call, an investor simply sells a call option without owning the underlying stock. If s/he writes a naked call & the stock goes up 100 or 200%, the writer has to deliver, but it is a high-risk strategy.

What is American contract?

An American option is a version of an options contract that allows holders to exercise the option rights at any time before and including the day of expiration.

What is an European contract?

A European contract only allows you to exercise on the day of expiration.

Which one is more profitable European contract or American contract?

An American contract option allows the investor to exercise any time before the expiration date whereas, in European contract options during their "exercise period" (usually right when they expire, but no earlier).

So an American style contract is exercised more but is it more profitable?

If I exercise my American contract before its expiration date, the investor might get more profit, but he/she might lose money too. Mathematically, there is no advantage, since an investor can make the same amount of profit on exercising its right on the day of its expiration.

When should you start options trading?

You should start options trading when you have enough investment and savings too. You need the proper knowledge, data, and strategies about the market. You should be able to not only predict but also implement the strategies at the right time.

How much should you invest in options trading?

It is advisable to start your investment with 5,000$ to 15,000$. Try not investing all of your savings or income on it since there is a high-risk factor involved in trading options.

When should you exercise your options?

According to Bill Bischoff, you should exercise your options put the very last-minute.

The last-minute is when the stock has risen to the point where you are ready to unload — or just before the option expiration date, whichever comes first. At the last minute or on the date of expiration, you know that there is no going higher than this, so you can easily exercise your options, although, on the last day, the tax cost is usually higher.

Best strategy of options trading?

According to Allen Everhart, there is no such thing is the best strategy. Everyday stock or market rate is different. Even the underlying asset or companies are different from each other too. You cannot apply one strategy to all of your options. However, all options trading strategies are directional.

What is a short put and long call strategy?

A short put and a long call are direction-ally the same. The shot put and the long call makes money when the stock goes up. But short put is known to be a little riskier than the long call strategy.

The short put can be exercised if the stock does not decline, and in that case, you can keep the premium of the option.

How an option writer makes money?

An option writer makes money when the stock or premium that has been bought reaches its expiration date without being exercised. In that case, the option writer gets to keep the entire premium.

How do investors lose money in options trading?

There is no one specific reason why an investor loses his/her money. There are different cases and scenarios. But the most common mistakes people make are they do not gather enough information or their lack of knowledge. Most people assume that it is a short way to become rich or may believe in "luck" too much.

CONCLUSION

Thank you for downloading this book. The objective of writing it was to let amateurs, novices, and even pros understand the tricky and sometimes hard to digest concepts.

The language of this book is, therefore, simple, easy, and user-friendly (in a sense that anyone can grab the meaning). On top of that, we have added as many examples as we could with each new concept so that the reader does not get confused.

In the end, we would wind up from where we began from – 'learning the concepts of options trading might seem difficult – but once you grab them – they are yours!"

So, just remember, you have got to be patient, risk-tolerant, and a mindful planner when it comes to business. Have a great trade. May each of your investments give you more profit than you expected.

www.ingramcontent.com/pod-product-compliance
Lightning Source LLC
Chambersburg PA
CBHW050250220526
45465CB00002B/629